W9-CTK-850

# TASCHEN's LONDON
*Shops*

Photos David Crookes
Text Christine Samuelian

# TASCHEN's LONDON
## Shops

Angelika Taschen

TASCHEN

# Shops

# James Purdey & Sons

Audley House
57–58 South Audley Street, London W1K 2ED
☎ +44 20 7499 1801
www.purdey.com
Tube: Bond Street/Green Park

Hunting may not be a palatable activity to some of us, but there are still plenty of Brits who take the sport very seriously, and Purdey has been around to indulge them since 1814 (the store has been on this site since 1882). Who knew there were so many types of game guns and rifles? Those with a weak stomach can leave the guns on the shelves and instead buy lots of tweed and some Wellingtons.

Nicht jedem sagt die Jagd zu. Doch viele Briten nehmen diesen Sport sehr ernst, und für sie ist Purdey das Paradies schlechthin. Seit 1814 gibt es dieses Geschäft bereits, allerdings erst seit 1882 an dieser Adresse. Man wird hier staunen, wie viele verschiedene Jagdgewehre es überhaupt gibt. Achtung: Wer schwache Nerven hat, sollte unverzüglich zu der zeitlosen Tweedbekleidung und den Gummistiefeln weiterziehen.

Tout le monde n'apprécie pas la chasse, mais de nombreux Britanniques prennent encore ce sport très au sérieux. Purdey est leur fournisseur depuis 1814 (la boutique actuelle existe depuis 1882). Qui aurait imaginé qu'il puisse y avoir une telle variété de fusils de chasse ? Les âmes sensibles préféreront sans doute se concentrer sur les beaux tweeds et les bottes en caoutchouc.

**Interior:** Tastefully conservative – with hunting trophies, oil paintings and old photographs of English gentlemen on the (genuine) fireplace mantelpiece.
**Open:** Mon–Fri 9.30am–5.30pm, Sat 10am–5pm.
**X-Factor:** Bespoke shotguns and rifles, such as the Purdey Sporter, as well as exclusive shooting clothing and accessories, e.g. tweeds, cashmere pullovers and safari fashion.

**Interieur:** Gediegen konservativ – mit Jagdtrophäen, Ölgemälden und alten Fotos englischer Gentlemen auf dem (echten!) Kamin.
**Öffnungszeiten:** Mo–Fr 9.30–17.30, Sa 10–17 Uhr.
**X-Faktor:** Maßangefertigte Jagdgewehre, wie den Purdey Sporter, außerdem exklusive Jagdkleidung und -accessoires, wie Tweedjacken, Kaschmirpullover und Safarimode.

**Intérieur :** Solidité et conservatisme, avec trophées de chasse, tableaux à l'huile et anciennes photos de gentilhommes anglais sur la (vraie !) cheminée.
**Horaires d'ouverture :** Lun–Ven 9h30– 17h30, Sam 10h–17h.
**Le « petit plus » :** Fabrication de fusils de chasse personnalisés. Également vêtements et accessoires de chasse, comme les vestes en tweed, les pullovers en cachemire et la mode safari.

# Stella McCartney

30 Bruton Street, London W1J 6QR
+44 20 7518 3100
www.stellamccartney.com
Tube: Bond Street/Green Park

She is the cool princess of the London fashion scene and what Stella McCartney sells in her shop is very much a reflection of her own personal style: a little bit sassy, a bit eclectic and very, very London. Her flattering tailored suits are hugely popular as are her feminine chiffon dresses, which normally come in very pale pinks and other neutrals. Also great are the leather-free handbags and shoes designed by the vegetarian. Lingerie, fragrances and an eco collection can also be found here.

Sie ist das Coolste, was die Londoner Modeszene zu bieten hat. Die Kleider und Accessoires, die Stella McCartney in ihrer Boutique verkauft, entsprechen genau ihrem persönlichen Stil: frech, eklektisch und typisch für London. Genauso beliebt wie die figurschmeichelnden Chiffonkleider in Blassrosa und anderen neutralen Tönen. Fantastisch auch die Taschen und Schuhe, die die Vegetarierin McCartney ohne Leder herstellen lässt. Außerdem findet man hier Parfüme, Dessous und eine Ökokollektion.

Dans sa boutique londonienne, la petite princesse de la mode anglaise présente des vêtements qui reflètent son propre sens du style : un peu provocants, éclectiques et très, très british. On s'arrache ses tailleurs impeccables et flatteurs ainsi que ses robes ultra féminines en mousseline de soie rose pâle ou dans d'autres couleurs neutres. Ses sacs et souliers sans cuir valent aussi le détour. On trouve ici aussi des parfums, de la lingerie et une collection écologique.

**Interior:** The shop interior, perfectly in keeping with the fashion, was created by Universal Design Studio.
**Open:** Mon–Sat 10am–6pm, Thu till 7pm.
**X-Factor:** The Stella McCartney kid's clothing line.

**Interieur:** Das perfekt zur Mode passende Shop-Interieur wurde von Universal Design Studio entworfen.
**Öffnungszeiten:** Mo–Sa 10–18, Do bis 19 Uhr.
**X-Faktor:** Stella McCartneys Kinderkollektion.

**Intérieur :** Universal Design Studio a conçu l'intérieur de la boutique en parfaite harmonie avec la mode présentée.
**Horaires d'ouverture :** Lun–Sam 10h–18h, Jeu jusqu'à 19h.
**Le « petit plus » :** La ligne de vêtements pour enfants de Stella McCartney.

# Holland & Holland

33 Bruton Street, London W1J 6HH
☎ +44 20 7499 4411
www.hollandandholland.com
Tube: Bond Street/Green Park

Harris Holland was originally a tobacconist – but in 1835 he made his hobby into his business and started producing firearms; he was so successful at this that he was permitted to include the word "royal" in the company name in 1885. Handmade rifles are still sold here, but the stylish country pursuit and safari fashion that was added to the portfolio in the 1990s is more suitable for everyday purposes. The ideal way to take the cashmere pullovers and tweed jackets home in style is to buy one of the elegant leather bags.

Eigentlich war Harris Holland Tabakhändler – doch 1835 machte er sein Hobby zum Beruf und gründete eine Manufaktur für Schusswaffen; er war damit so erfolgreich, dass er den Firmennamen 1885 um den Zusatz „Royal" ergänzen durfte. Handgefertigte Gewehre gibt es hier noch immer – etwas alltagstauglicher ist aber die schicke Safari- und Countrystyle Mode, die in den 1990ern ins Portfolio aufgenommen wurde. Um die Kaschmirpullis und Tweedjacken stilvoll nach Hause zu bringen, ersteht man am besten auch eine der eleganten Ledertaschen.

Harris Holland était marchand de tabac, mais il aimait la chasse. En 1835, faisant de son violon d'Ingres un métier, il fonda une manufacture d'armes à feu. Celle-ci connut un tel succès qu'il put accoler, en 1885, l'adjectif « Royal » au nom de sa maison. On trouve encore ici des fusils fabriqués à la main, mais la ligne de vêtements chics de style safari et country, développée au cours des années 1990, est plus adaptée à la vie de tous les jours. Pour rapporter chez soi les pulls en cachemire et les vestes en tweed, un des élégants sacs en cuir s'impose.

**Interior:** The stuffed animals, oil paintings and historical photographs in the salesrooms recall British heritage.
**Open:** Mon–Fri 9am–6pm, Sat 10am–5pm.
**X-Factor:** The legendary "Paradox" gun. The luxury bespoke service.

**Interieur:** In den Verkaufsräumen erinnern ausgestopfte Tiere, Ölbilder und historische Fotos an die britische Kolonialgeschichte.
**Öffnungszeiten:** Mo–Fr 9–18, Sa 10–17 Uhr.
**X-Faktor:** Das legendäre „Paradox"-Gewehr. Die luxuriösen Maßanfertigungen.

**Intérieur :** Dans les pièces, les animaux empaillés, les toiles et les photos historiques rappellent le passé colonial de l'Angleterre.
**Horaires d'ouverture :** Lun–Ven 9h–18h, Sam 10h–17h.
**Le « petit plus » :** L'arme légendaire « Paradox ». Les sur-mesure luxeux.

# Matthew Williamson

28 Bruton Street, London W1J 6QH
☏ +44 20 7629 6200
www.matthewwilliamson.com
Tube: Bond Street/Green Park

Matthew Williamson is one of the darlings of the British fashion landscape. He burst on to the scene in the late 1990s with his Indian-inspired colourful fabrics worn by model friends such as Jade Jagger. His look has moved on but his popularity hasn't diminished. His jewel box of a store with his rich colours and striking details is an ode to his particular – and lasting – sense of style.

Matthew Williamson gehört zu den Lieblingen der britischen Modeszene. Auf ihn aufmerksam wurde sie in den späten 1990ern, als Leute wie Jade Jagger anfingen, seine bunten, damals indisch angehauchten Kreationen zu tragen. Sein Look hat sich weiterentwickelt, angesagt ist er genauso wie damals. Seine farbenfrohe Boutique mit vielen interessanten Details erinnert an eine Schmuckschatulle und ist eine Ode an seine eigenwillige Ästhetik.

Matthew Williamson est un des chouchous de la mode anglaise. Il a fait sensation à la fin des années 1990 avec ses tissus aux couleurs indiennes portés par ses amies mannequins, comme Jade Jagger. Son style a changé, mais pas sa popularité. Sa boutique, un petit bijou rempli de couleurs et de détails, est un hommage à son sens esthétique unique.

**Interior:** According to Suzy Menkes, this boutique is like a bird of paradise – the interior is as wonderfully colourful as the collections.
**Open:** Mon–Sat 10am–6pm (Thu till 7pm).
**X-Factor:** Helena Christensen and Sienna Miller are regular customers here.

**Interieur:** Diese Boutique gleiche einem Paradiesvogel, schrieb Suzy Menkes – das Interieur ist so fantastisch bunt wie die Kollektionen.
**Öffnungszeiten:** Mo–Sa 10–18 Uhr (Do bis 19 Uhr).
**X-Faktor:** Helena Christensen und Sienna Miller sind Stammkundinnen.

**Intérieur :** Suzy Menkes a écrit que cette boutique ressemblait à un oiseau de paradis, sa décoration est aussi colorée que ses collections.
**Horaires d'ouverture :** Lun–Sam 10h–18h (Jeu jusqu'à 19h).
**Le « petit plus » :** Helena Christensen et Sienna Miller sont de fidèles clientes.

# Smythson

40 New Bond Street, London W1S 2DE
☎ +44 20 7629 8558
www.smythson.com
Tube: Bond Street/Oxford Circus

Started in 1887, Smythson has been the purveyor of fine products for those who love stationery. It is the most quintessentially English place in London to get your thank-you cards, bespoke stationery, beautiful pens, leather goods, travel and business accessories. Do not leave the premises without a classic travel wallet. It's as beautiful as it is practical.

Smythson ist seit 1887 Lieferant für edle Schreibwaren und Briefpapiere. Hier kann man Dankeskarten, individuell bedrucktes Briefpapier, edle Schreibstifte und Lederwaren sowie Reise- und Business-Accessoires beziehen – alles in feinster englischer Tradition. Unbedingt eine der Classic-Travel-Brieftaschen erstehen: Sie sind nicht nur schön zum Anschauen, sondern auch äußerst praktisch.

Depuis 1887, Smythson approvisionne les amateurs de beau papier. C'est l'endroit à Londres où acheter ses cartes de remerciement, son papier à en-tête, de beaux stylos et des articles en cuir, ainsi que des accessoires de voyage et de business. Ne repartez pas sans un portefeuille de voyage, ils sont aussi beaux que pratiques.

**Interior:** Classical elegance, in timeless black, gray and white.
**Open:** Mon, Tue, Wed, Fri 9.30am–6pm, Thu 10am–7pm, Sat 10am–6pm.
**X-Factor:** The attractive souvenirs: little notebooks with names like "Yummy Mummy", "Keep Calm and Carry On" or "Make it Happen" printed on them.

**Interieur:** Klassisch elegant; in zeitlosem Schwarz-Grau-Weiß gehalten.
**Öffnungszeiten:** Mo, Di, Mi, Fr 9.30–18, Do 10–19, Sa 10–18 Uhr.
**X-Faktor:** Schöne Souvenirs sind die Notizbüchlein mit Titeln wie „Yummy Mummy", „Keep Calm and Carry On" oder „Make it Happen".

**Intérieur :** Élégante et classique ; en couleurs intemporelles de noir, gris, blanc.
**Horaires d'ouverture :** Lun, Mar, Mer, Ven 9h30–18h, Jeu 10h–19h, Sam 10h–18h.
**Le « petit plus » :** Les calepins aux titres de « Yummy Mummy », « Keep Calm and Carry On » ou « Make it Happen » seront de jolis souvenirs.

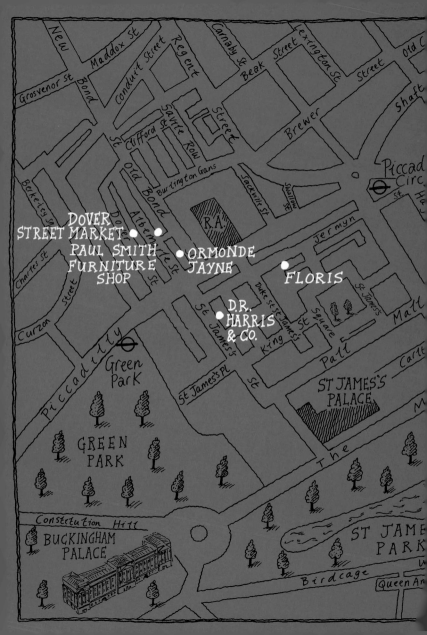

# Ormonde Jayne

The Royal Arcade
28 Old Bond Street, London W1S 4SL
☎ +44 20 7499 1100
www.ormondejayne.com
Tube: Green Park

Linda Pilkington founded this divine little perfumery in 2003 with an aim to sell gorgeous, luxury scents. The shop is located in the beautiful Victorian Royal Arcade built in the 1880s. All of her perfumes are made in London and her perfume library boasts scents inspired by her worldwide travels. Walk out with a new signature scent or just pick up perfumed candles as wonderful gifts.

Linda Pilkington bietet in dieser 2003 von ihr gegründeten Parfümerie wunderbare Luxusdüfte an, und das mitten in dem wunderschönen Bau der viktorianischen Royal Arcade aus den 1880ern. Alle Parfüms werden in London hergestellt; dazu gibt es eine Parfüm-Bibliothek mit Düften, inspiriert von Pilkingtons Reisen rund um die Welt. Einen der neuen Düfte zu erwerben ist ein Muss, und die Duftkerzen geben schöne Geschenke her.

Linda Pilkington a ouvert cette charmante petite parfumerie en 2003 afin d'y vendre ses fragrances luxueuses. Elle est située dans les belles Royal Arcades victoriennes, une galerie bâtie vers 1880. Tous ses parfums sont fabriqués à Londres et beaucoup s'inspirent de ses voyages à travers le monde. Repartez avec votre nouveau parfum ou simplement des bougies parfumées qui font des cadeaux divins.

**Interior:** The luxuriously dramatic atmosphere conjured up by the brilliant black glass is the work of Caulder Moore.
**Open:** Mon–Sat 10am–6pm.
**X-Factor:** Even the shower creams and bath oils have exotic aromas – Frangipani being particularly fragrant.

**Interieur:** Das luxuriös-dramatische Ambiente aus glänzendem schwarzen Glas stammt von Caulder Moore.
**Öffnungszeiten:** Mo–Sa 10–18 Uhr.
**X-Faktor:** Auch die Duschcremes und Badeöle haben exotische Aromen – besonders gut riecht Frangipani.

**Intérieur :** Caulder Moore a créé cette ambiance luxueuse et dramatique en verre noir brillant.
**Horaires d'ouverture :** Lun–Sam 10h–18h.
**Le « petit plus » :** Les crèmes de douche et les huiles de bain ont, elles aussi, des arômes exotiques, celui à la frangipane sent particulièrement bon.

# Paul Smith Furniture Shop

9 Albemarle Street, London W1S 4BL
☎ +44 20 7493 4565
www.paulsmith.co.uk
Tube: Green Park

As with Sir Paul Smith's fashion collections, the furniture he peddles has his quirky British modern twist (and humour) all over it. He opened this funky shop opposite Brown's Hotel in 2005 and he showcases pieces of contemporary furniture jazzed up with interesting fabrics or older pieces modernised with his own textiles. Colourful china, the ones in Smith's signature stripes, are also cool.

Genau wie seine Mode ist die Möbelkollektion von Sir Paul Smith eigenwillig britisch und humorvoll. Das unkonventionelle Geschäft gleich gegenüber dem Brown's Hotel eröffnete er 2005. Hier gibt es mit interessanten Stoffen aufgepeppte Möbel, aber auch gebrauchte Stücke, die mit Smith-Textilien zu neuem Leben erweckt wurden. Cool ist auch das bunte Porzellangeschirr mit den typischen Paul-Smith-Streifen.

Comme sa mode, les meubles choisis par Sir Paul Smith possèdent cette touche d'excentricité et d'humour toute britannique. Dans cette boutique ouverte en face du Brown's Hotel en 2005, il présente des meubles contemporains, égayés par des tissus intéressants ou des pièces plus anciennes modernisées avec ses propres textiles. On y trouve aussi de jolies porcelaines aux rayures typiquement Paul Smith.

**Interior:** Two rooms that are entirely different in design – simplicity and minimalism vs. antique market.
**Open:** Mon, Tue, Wed, Fri 10.30am–6pm, Thu 10.30am–7pm, Sat 10am–6pm.
**X-Factor:** Rare and ever-changing objects, including antique furniture reupholstered in Paul Smith fabrics. Sir Paul Smith offers a continually changing collection of extraordinary furniture, art and curios from around the world.

**Interieur:** Zwei Räume in völlig unterschiedlichen Designs – Schlichtheit und Minimalismus vs. Antikmarkt.
**Öffnungszeiten:** Mo, Di, Mi, Fr 10.30–18, Do 10.30–19, Sa 10–18 Uhr.
**X-Faktor:** Seltene und immer wechselnde Objekte, u. a. Vintage-Möbel, die mit Paul-Smith-Stoffen neu bezogen werden. Sir Paul Smith bietet eine Kollektion außergewöhnlicher Möbel, Kunstwerke und Kuriositäten aus der ganzen Welt.

**Intérieur :** Deux pièces au design complètement différent – sobriété et minimalisme contre marché d'antiquités.
**Horaires d'ouverture :** Lun, Mar, Mer, Ven 10h30–18h, Jeu 10h30–19h, Sam 10h–18h.
**Le « petit plus » :** Objets rares et meubles vintage retapissés avec des tissus Paul-Smith. Sir Paul Smith propose une collection exceptionnelle de meubles, œuvres d'art et curiosités venant du monde entier.

# Dover Street Market

17–18 Dover Street, London W1S 4LT
☎ +44 20 7518 0680
www.doverstreetmarket.com
Tube: Green Park

Started by Comme des Garçons in 2004, it is more like a museum. In the so-called Tachiagari the interior is completely transformed by different designers to reflect the new collections of the season. Fashion is exhibited here, not merely hung up for customers to admire. This is where Raf Simons displayed his creations in an environment designed by Jan De Cock. Brands include big names such as Lanvin and Alaïa but more obscure labels (Sacai Gem and egg) are well served too.

Eigentlich ist Dover Street Market mehr ein Museum als ein Geschäft. Von Comme des Garçons 2004 ins Leben gerufen, werden hier Kleider wie Ausstellungsstücke präsentiert. Beim so genannten Tachiagari wird das Interieur von verschiedenen Designern komplett neu gestaltet, um die Ideen der aktuellen Kollektionen der Saison widerzuspiegeln. So zeigte Raf Simons seine Kreationen in einer vom Künstler Jan De Cock gestalteten Umgebung. Neben anderen großen Namen wie Lanvin und Alaïa findet man hier auch weniger bekannte Labels wie Sacai Gem und egg.

Lancé par Comme des Garçons en 2004, c'est plus un musée où les clients peuvent admirer la mode présentée dans différents environnements. Dans le fameux Tachiagari, l'intérieur est intégralement redécoré par différents designers afin de refléter les idées des collections de la saison actuelle. C'est ainsi que Raf Simons a montré ses créations dans un environnement aménagé par l'artiste Jan De Cock. On y trouve de grands créateurs comme Lanvin ou Alaïa, mais aussi des marques plus obscures telles que Sacai Gem ou egg.

**Interior:** The original concept is by Rei Kawakubo with alternating spaces such as the bag-and-shoe space entitled "Burnt Ballroom" by installation artist Andy Hillman.
**Open:** Mon–Wed 11am–6.30pm, Thu–Sat 11am–7pm, Sun midday–5pm.
**X-Factor:** Take a shopping break at the fourth-floor Rose Bakery and enjoy cakes, quiches and tea.

**Interieur:** Das ursprüngliche Konzept stammt von Rei Kawakubo mit wechselnden Räumen wie dem „Burnt Ballroom", einem Taschen-und-Schuh-Raum von Installationskünstler Andy Hillman.
**Öffnungszeiten:** Mo–Mi 11–18.30, Do–Sa 11–19, So 12–17 Uhr.
**X-Faktor:** In der Rose Bakery im 4. Stock kann man bei Kuchen, Quiche oder Tee eine Shoppingpause einlegen.

**Intérieur :** Le concept d'origine est de Rei Kawakubo avec différents espaces tel que celui consacré aux sacs et chaussures, une installation intitulée « salle de bal brûlée » de l'artiste Andy Hillman.
**Horaires d'ouverture :** Lun–Mer 11h–18h30, Jeu–Sam 11h–19h, Dim 12h–17h.
**Le « petit plus » :** Une pause shopping à la Rose Bakery (4e étage) s'impose pour déguster du thé, ou un gâteau.

# D.R. Harris & Co.

29 St James's Street, London SW1A 1HB
☎ +44 20 7930 3915
www.drharris.co.uk
Tube: Green Park

D.R. Harris was established in St James's in 1790, when the area was known as Clubland because of the many gentlemen's clubs located here. This traditional pharmacy holds a royal warrant as chemist for HRH The Prince of Wales. Customers come in for the all-natural skincare products – some made from recipes that are 125 years old – and for badger-hair brushes.

Als D.R. Harris 1790 in St James's gegründet wurde, nannte man diese Gegend wegen der vielen ansässigen Herrenklubs „Clubland". Die traditionelle Apotheke ist königlicher Hoflieferant des Prinzen von Wales und hat sich vor allem mit natürlichen Hautpflegeprodukten, die heute noch aus zum Teil 125 Jahre alten Rezepten hergestellt werden, einen Namen gemacht. Bei D.R. Harris findet man auch Bürsten aus echtem Dachshaar.

D.R. Harris est établi à St James's depuis 1790, quand le quartier était surnommé Clubland en raison des nombreux clubs de gentlemen. Cette pharmacie traditionnelle est le fournisseur attitré de S.A.R. le prince de Galles. On vient y chercher ses cosmétiques 100% naturels (certains confectionnés à partir de recettes vieilles de 125 ans) et ses blaireaux de barbier.

**Interior:** In one of London's oldest pharmacies the products are still presented in antique display cases and shelves.
**Open:** Mon–Fri 8.30am–6pm, Sat 9.30am–5pm.
**X-Factor:** The handmade brushes, shaving sets, creams and soaps make charmingly old-fashioned gifts for the modern man.

**Interieur:** Die Nähe zum Adel verpflichtet: In einer der ältesten Pharmazien Londons werden die Produkte noch immer in den antiken Vitrinen und Regalen präsentiert.
**Öffnungszeiten:** Mo–Fr 8.30–18, Sa 9.30–17 Uhr.
**X-Faktor:** Die handgefertigten Bürsten, Rasiersets und -seifen sowie Cremes sind herrlich altmodische Geschenke für den modernen Mann.

**Intérieur :** Noblesse à proximité oblige : dans l'une des plus anciennes pharmacies de Londres on présente encore les articles dans des vitrines et des étagères surannées.
**Horaires d'ouverture :** Lun–Ven 8h30–18h, Sam 9h30–17h.
**Le « petit plus » :** Les brosses, trousses de rasages et savons maison sont de merveilleux cadeaux désuets pour l'homme d'aujourd'hui.

# Floris

89 Jermyn Street, London SW1Y 6JH
☎ +44 20 7930 2885
www.florislondon.com
Tube: Green Park/Piccadilly Circus

Though the staff at Floris, founded in 1730, will no longer iron the banknotes before handing you your change, as they did in the 19th century, they will present it to you on a velvet-covered tray. Floris fragrances have been worn by British monarchs since 1820, as well as by such luminaries as Noël Coward and Eva Perón. The sandalwood scent is particularly lovely.

Im 19. Jahrhundert pflegte das Personal beim 1730 gegründeten Parfümeur Floris die Banknoten zu bügeln, bevor sie den Kunden überreicht wurden. Diese Zeiten sind zwar vorbei, doch das Wechselgeld wird heute – immer noch stilvoll – auf einem samtbezogenen Tablett übergeben. Seit 1820 haben britische Monarchen und auch illustre Namen wie Noël Coward und Eva Perón die Düfte von Floris getragen. Besonders fein riecht der Sandelholzduft.

On n'y repasse plus les billets avant de vous rendre la monnaie comme au XIXᵉ siècle, mais elle vous est quand même tendue sur un plateau en velours. Fondé en 1730, Floris parfume les monarques britanniques depuis 1820 et a compté parmi ses clients des célébrités telles que Noël Coward et Eva Perón. Son santal est particulièrement divin.

**Interior:** The wonderful display cases are made of Spanish mahogany and were crafted in 1851 on the occasion of the First World Exhibition in London.
**Open:** Mon–Fri 9.30am–6pm, Sat 10am–6pm.
**X-Factor:** In 1730 Juan Famenias Floris left Menorca for England, where he opened a hair-dressing shop – which has become a perfume empire.

**Interieur:** Die wunderschönen Vitrinen sind aus spanischem Mahagoni und wurden 1851 anlässlich der ersten Weltausstellung in London gefertigt.
**Öffnungszeiten:** Mo–Fr 9.30–18, Sa 10–18 Uhr.
**X-Faktor:** 1730 kam Juan Famenias Floris aus Menorca nach England und eröffnete einen Friseurladen – daraus ist ein Duftimperium geworden.

**Intérieur :** Les magnifiques vitrines sont en acajou espagnol et ont été fabriquées en 1851, à l'occasion de la la première Exposition universelle organisée à Londres.
**Horaires d'ouverture :** Lun–Ven 9h30–18h, Sam 10h–18h.
**Le « petit plus » :** En 1730, Juan Famenias Floris quitta Minorque pour l'Angleterre où il ouvrit un salon de coiffure, devenu aujourd'hui un empire du parfum.

# Penhaligon's

41 Wellington Street, London WC2E 7BN
☎ +44 20 7836 2150
www.penhaligons.com
Tube: Covent Garden

Classic scents in beautiful packaging is the essence of what this shop is about. The company was founded in 1870 by William Henry Penhaligon, who came to London from Penzance to become a barber, but found himself selling perfumed waters and pomades to the aristocracy. Kate Moss's favourite is Bluebell. Treat yourself to the citrusy Blenheim Bouquet scent, created in 1902, in the beautiful glass bottle.

Penhaligon's, das sind klassische Düfte in wunderschöner Verpackung. Das Geschäft wurde 1870 von William Henry Penhaligon gegründet, der, weil er Friseur werden wollte, von Penzance, Cornwall, nach London zog. Friseur wurde er dann doch nicht. Stattdessen verkaufte er der Aristokratie parfümierte Wasser und Pomaden, und 1902 schuf er den Zitrusduft Blenheim Bouquet. Der Lieblingsduft von Kate Moss ist Bluebell. Wer sich verwöhnen will, sollte eines der traumhaft schönen Glasflakons erstehen.

Des fragrances classiques superbement présentées. La maison a été fondée par William Henry Penhaligon en 1870, venu de Penzance pour devenir barbier, mais qui se retrouva vendant des eaux parfumées et des pommades à l'aristocratie de Londres. Le parfum favori de Kate Moss est Bluebell. Faites-vous plaisir avec le Blenheim Bouquet, aux senteurs citriques, créé en 1902 et vendu dans un magnifique flacon en verre.

**Interior:** Luxurious British understatement at its best: display cases, mirrors and parquet flooring all highly polished.
**Open:** Mon–Wed 10am–6pm, Thu–Sat 10am–7pm, Sun midday–6pm.
**X-Factor:** The Hammam Bouquet first created in 1872 is still sold today.

**Interieur:** Luxuriös-britisches Understatement at its best: Vitrinen, Spiegel und Parkett sind auf Hochglanz poliert.
**Öffnungszeiten:** Mo–Mi 10–18, Do–Sa 10–19, So 12–18 Uhr.
**X-Faktor:** Bis heute kann man hier die erste Kreation Hammam Bouquet von 1872 kaufen.

**Intérieur :** Understatement luxueux et britannique dans toute sa splendeur : vitrines, miroirs et parquet brillent de mille feux.
**Horaires d'ouverture :** Lun–Mer 10h–18h, Jeu–Sam 10h–19h, Dim 12h–18h.
**Le « petit plus » :** On peut encore acheter Hammam Bouquet, la toute première création de 1872.

# Agent Provocateur

6 Broadwick Street, London W1F 8HL
☎ +44 20 7439 0229
www.agentprovocateur.com
Tube: Tottenham Court Road/Oxford Circus

Soho has always had a risqué reputation, but it's seldom as stylishly executed as at Agent Provocateur. The emphasis is on vintage styles and a saucy, tongue-in-cheek eroticism, as evidenced in the pale pink house coats worn by the sales girls and the naughty tableaux in the windows.

Gewagtes fand man in Soho schon immer. Doch so richtig stilvoll wird es erst beim Dessous-Geschäft Agent Provocateur. Vintage-Look wird hier mit frech-ironischer Erotik umgesetzt, kesse Verkäuferinnen tragen blassrosafarbene Kittel, und im Schaufenster hängen leicht anzügliche Bilder.

Soho a toujours eu une réputation de quartier chaud, mais le libertinage a rarement été aussi chic que chez Agent Provocateur. Le style rétro est à l'honneur ainsi que l'érotisme coquin et ironique, comme en attestent les blouses rose pâle des vendeuses et les tableaux grivois en vitrine.

**Interior:** The shop is in pale pink and black. The boudoir-style fitting rooms are a highlight.
**Open:** Mon–Wed, Fri/Sat 11am–7pm, Thu 11am–8pm, Sun midday–5pm.
**X-Factor:** The sales staff's shop coats were designed by Vivienne Westwood.

**Interieur:** Der Shop ist in Blassrosa und Schwarz gehalten; Highlights sind die Umkleidekabinen im Boudoir-Stil.
**Öffnungszeiten:** Mo–Mi, Fr/Sa 11–19, Do 11–20, So 12–17 Uhr.
**X-Faktor:** Die Kittelkleider der Verkäuferinnen entwarf Vivienne Westwood.

**Intérieur :** La boutique est tout en rose clair et noir ; les highlights sont les cabines d'essayage dans le style d'un boudoir.
**Horaires d'ouverture :** Lun–Mer, Ven/Sam 11h–19h, Jeu 11h–20h, Dim 12h–17h.
**Le « petit plus » :** C'est Vivienne Westwood qui a dessiné les blouses des vendeuses.

# Liberty

Regent Street, London W1B 5AH
☎ +44 20 7734 1234
www.liberty.co.uk
Tube: Oxford Circus

With its Tudor façade, signature floral prints and mellow wood interior, Liberty is one of the more old-fashioned of London's department stores. But don't let that fool you: the shopping here is second to none. It has an ever-changing selection of new and exciting labels, as well as a fantastic interiors section with vintage and classic designs mixed in with newer ones.

Mit einer Fassade im Tudor-Stil und behaglichem Blumenmuster- und Holzdekor gehört Liberty zu den Kaufhäusern der altmodischen Sorte. Doch von solchen Äußerlichkeiten sollte man sich nicht täuschen lassen. Hier gibt's die neuesten und aufregendsten Labels und eine fantastische Interior-Abteilung mit Vintage-Möbeln und Designklassikern zusammen mit ein paar neuen Entwürfen.

Avec sa façade Tudor, ses imprimés fleuris et ses boiseries patinées, Liberty a un charme désuet, mais ne vous y trompez pas : c'est un paradis du shopping. Sa sélection de nouvelles marques intéressantes est constamment renouvelée et son formidable rayon décoration mêle le classique et le vintage aux dernières créations.

**Interior:** The striking building dating from the 1920s is by Edwin T. Hall and his son Edwin S. Hall. The wood used for the magnificent panelling inside is from the two legendary ships HMS Impregnable and HMS Hindustan.
**Open:** Mon–Sat 10am–9pm, Sun midday–6pm.
**X-Factor:** The concierge at Liberty knows not only the shop but can also recommend the best restaurants and cafés nearby.

**Interieur:** Das markante Gebäude bauten Edwin T. Hall und sein Sohn Edwin S. Hall in den 1920ern. Für die herrliche Vertäfelung im Inneren verwendeten sie das Holz der beiden legendären Schiffe HMS Impregnable und HMS Hindustan.
**Öffnungszeiten:** Mo–Sa 10–21, So 12–18 Uhr.
**X-Faktor:** Der Liberty-Concierge kennt nicht nur das Kaufhaus sehr gut, sondern verrät auch die besten Restaurants und Cafés in der Nähe.

**Intérieur :** Ce remarquable bâtiment a été construit par Edwin T. Hall et son fils Edwin S. Hall dans les années 1920. Pour les magnifiques boiseries à l'intérieur ils ont utilisé le bois des deux navires légendaires, le HMS Impregnable et le HMS Hindustan.
**Horaires d'ouverture :** Lun–Sam 10h–21h, Dim 12h–18h.
**Le « petit plus » :** Le concierge connaît non seulement le magasin, mais révèle aussi les meilleurs restaurants et cafés du quartier.

# Topshop

214–216 Oxford Street, London W1D 1LA
☎ +44 8448 487 487
www.topshop.com
Tube: Oxford Circus

No visit to London is complete without a stop at Topshop's flagship store. If it was on the runway, you'll find an affordable version of it here, along with a nail bar and a café. Expectant mothers can also keep up to date with Topshop's maternity range. If you're having trouble finding what you want, consult one of the resident style advisers, who'll be happy to scour the rails for you.

Ohne einen Abstecher in den Topshop-Flagship-Store gemacht zu haben, kann man London unmöglich verlassen. Hier findet man eine erschwingliche Version von Laufstegmode, eine Nagelpflege-Bar und ein Café. Auch werdende Mütter müssen nicht auf die letzten Trends verzichten: Die Umstandskleidung ist modisch. Praktisch: die Topshop-Style-Berater, die für ihre Kunden nach den passenden Stücken suchen.

Une visite à Londres ne serait pas complète sans un passage par la boutique phare de Topshop. Vous y trouverez toutes les nouvelles tendances à des prix abordables, ainsi qu'un nail bar et un café. Les futures mamans ne seront pas en reste grâce à une section maternité branchée. Si vous êtes perdu, des conseillers en style vous aideront à parcourir les rayons.

**Interior:** This flagship store is also the chain's largest: 90000 square feet presented in ever-changing designs.
**Open:** Mon, Tue, Wed, Sat 9am–8pm, Thu/Fri 9am–10pm, Sun 11.30–6pm.
**X-Factor:** The online shop.

**Interieur:** Der Flagship-Store ist zugleich der größte der Kette – er umfasst 8400 immer wieder neu gestaltete Quadratmeter.
**Öffnungszeiten:** Mo, Di, Mi, Sa 9–20, Do/Fr 9–22, So 11.30–18 Uhr.
**X-Faktor:** Der Onlineshop.

**Intérieur :** Le Flagship Store est le plus grand de la chaîne avec ses 8400 mètres carrés constamment redécorés.
**Horaires d'ouverture :** Lun, Mar, Mer, Sam 9h–20h, Jeu/Ven 9h–22h, Dim 11h30–18h.
**Le « petit plus » :** La boutique Internet.

# Neal's Yard Remedies

15 Neal's Yard, London WC2H 9DP
☏ +44 20 7379 7222
www.nealsyardremedies.com
Tube: Covent Garden

Neal's Yard Remedies, a charming little shop, was opened in a hippy dippy courtyard in 1981. Surrounded by groovy hair salons, tattoo parlours and vegetarian restaurants, the company has stuck to its philosophy of providing natural, organic, handmade remedies and cosmetics using its own herbs grown in Dorset. The signature blue bottles are as practical as they are pretty: they cut down 97% of UV light and protect the sensitive herbal extracts.

Neal's Yard Remedies wurde 1981 in diesem alternativen Hinterhof gegründet und ist heute von coolen Hair-Salons, Tattoo-Shops und vegetarischen Restaurants umgeben. Das Unternehmen stellt natürliche, handgemachte Bio-Heilmittel und -Pflegeprodukte aus eigens dafür angebauten Kräutern in Dorset her. Die dunkelblauen Fläschchen sind praktisch – sie schützen die empfindlichen Kräuterextrakte vor UV-Strahlung – und sind schön anzuschauen.

Neal's Yard Remedies a ouvert sa charmante boutique en 1981 dans cette cour aux accents baba cool. Entourée de salons de coiffure branchés, d'échoppes de tatoueurs et de restaurants végétariens, elle est restée fidèle à sa philosophie : proposer des produits naturels, bios et artisanaux à base de ses propres herbes cultivées dans le Dorset. Aussi jolis que pratiques, ses flacons bleus protègent les extraits végétaux des UV.

**Interior:** The façade is colourful, while the shop interior is simple; the most important things here are the products. Good feng shui.
**Open:** Mon–Sat 10am–7pm (Thu till 7.30pm), Sun 11am–6pm.
**X-Factor:** The therapy rooms next door, where a wide range of massages, acupuncture, homeopathy and flower-essence therapy are available.

**Interieur:** So bunt die Fassade ist, so schlicht gibt sich der Shop selbst – das Wichtigste sind hier die Produkte. Gutes Feng Shui.
**Öffnungszeiten:** Mo–Sa 10–19 (Do bis 19.30), So 11–18 Uhr.
**X-Faktor:** Die Therapy Rooms nebenan mit vielfältigem Angebot von Massagen über Akupunktur zu Homöopathie und Blütenessenz-Therapie.

**Intérieur :** Autant la façade est colorée, autant la boutique est sobre ; le plus important ici sont les produits. Bon Feng Shui.
**Horaires d'ouverture :** Lun–Sam 10h–19h (Jeu jusqu'à 19h30), Dim 11h–18h.
**Le « petit plus » :** Les Therapy Rooms avec leur offre diversifiée qui va des massages à l'homéopathie et l'aromathérapie en passant par l'acupuncture.

# Neal's Yard Dairy

17 Shorts Gardens, London WC2H 9AT
☎ +44 20 7240 5700
www.nealsyarddairy.co.uk
Tube: Covent Garden

If you love cheese, you'll love Neal's Yard Dairy. Since opening in 1979, it's been providing Londoners with all-natural, handmade cheeses and yoghurts by independent regional farmers. You can get everything here from Italian-style Mozzarella di Bufala to a Gloucestershire favourite known as Stinking Bishop. All the Dairy's cheeses are seasonal, so you may not find what you came in for – but you'll no doubt find something just as good.

Neal's Yard Dairy ist ein Schlaraffenland für Liebhaber britischer Käsesorten. Seit 1979 werden hier Londoner mit handgemachtem Käse und Joghurt aus natürlichen Zutaten von unabhängigen regionalen Farmern verwöhnt. Ob ein Mozzarella di bufala oder ein Stinking Bishop aus Gloucestershire – das Angebot ist riesig. Die Käse werden saisonal hergestellt, deshalb findet man nicht immer, was man sucht. Ein Ersatz wird aber garantiert genauso gut schmecken.

Amateurs de fromages, Neal's Yard Dairy est faite pour vous. Depuis 1979, cette boutique approvisionne les Londoniens en fromages et yaourts naturels maison, provenant de fermes indépendantes de la région. Le choix va de la mozzarella de buffle à « l'évê que puant », une spécialité du Gloucestershire. Les produits étant saisonniers, vous n'y trouverez peut-être pas ce que vous cherchez, mais vous ressortirez certainement avec autre chose d'aussi bon.

**Interior:** The cheeses are stacked on a simple counter – very picturesque and very enticing.
**Open:** Mon–Sat 10am–7pm.
**X-Factor:** Only regional cheeses from Great Britain and Ireland, which ripen in the rooms of Neal's Yard Dairy in Bermondsey under brick railway arches.

**Interieur:** Auf einer einfachen Theke stapeln sich die Käselaibe – sehr malerisch und sehr verlockend duftend.
**Öffnungszeiten:** Mo–Sa 10–19 Uhr.
**X-Faktor:** Ausschließlich regionale Käse aus Großbritannien und Irland, die in den Räumen von Neal's Yard Dairy unter Bahngleisbögen in Bermondsey reifen.

**Intérieur :** Les meules de fromages sont empilées sur un comptoir tout simple : très pittoresque et délicieusement odorant.
**Horaires d'ouverture :** Lun–Sam 10h–19h.
**Le « petit plus » :** Exclusivement des fromages régionaux de Grande-Bretagne et d'Irlande qui sont portés à maturité dans les locaux de Neal's Yard Dairy à Bermondsey.

# James Smith & Sons

Hazelwood House
53 New Oxford Street, London WC1A 1BL
☎ +44 20 7836 4731
www.james-smith.co.uk
Tube: Tottenham Court Road

James Smith & Sons, established in 1830, is where to turn when the British weather does what it does best: pour with rain. Locals go to this legendary shop – and have done so since 1857 – for handmade umbrellas and walking sticks, many of which are still made at their New Oxford Street premises. There are few London rituals so time-honoured as a visit to Smith's, rain or shine. And its classic walking sticks make great souvenirs.

Zeigt sich das britische Wetter von seiner besten Seite und schickt wieder mal Regen, sollte man James Smith & Sons, gegründet 1830, aufsuchen. Die Leute aus dem Viertel kommen in diesen legendären Laden – und zwar seit 1857 –, um handgefertigte Regenschirme und Spazierstöcke zu kaufen, die häufig noch in der Werkstatt auf der New Oxford Street produziert werden. Es gibt wenige Rituale, die den Lauf der Zeit so überstehen wie der Besuch bei Smith & Sons. Zu den Klassikern gehören die Gehstöcke: Sie sind super Geschenke.

Quand le climat anglais est fidèle à sa réputation, à savoir quand il pleut, James Smith & Sons, fondé en 1830, est l'endroit où aller. Depuis 1857, les Londoniens s'approvisionnent dans cette boutique légendaire en parapluies et en cannes, dont la plupart sont toujours fabriqués artisanalement dans leurs ateliers de New Oxford Street. Même si le soleil est au rendez-vous, une visite chez Smith est un rituel londonien. Ses cannes classiques font de beaux cadeaux.

**Interior:** The interior retains most of its original features, unchanged since the late 19th century.
**Open:** Mon–Fri 9.30am–5.15pm, Sat 10am–5.15pm.
**X-Factor:** Umbrellas made by Smith's can be expertly repaired and restored by them.

**Interieur:** Der aus dem späten 19. Jahrhundert stammende Innenraum ist zum größten Teil original erhalten.
**Öffnungszeiten:** Mo–Fr 9.30–17.15, Sa 10–17.15 Uhr.
**X-Faktor:** Regenschirme von Smith's können von ihnen repariert und fachmännisch wiederhergestellt werden.

**Intérieur :** L'intérieur conserve la plupart de son décor d'origine datant de la fin du XIX$^e$ siècle.
**Horaires d'ouverture :** Lun–Ven 9h30–17h15, Sam 10h–17h15.
**Le « petit plus » :** Smith's répare et restaure avec art les parapluies fabriqués par ses ateliers.

# The London Silver Vaults

Chancery House
53–64 Chancery Lane, London WC2A 1QS
☎ +44 20 7242 3844
www.thesilvervaults.com
Tube: Chancery Lane

With more than 30 dealers hawking everything from thimbles to elaborate candelabra, you can bet that if it's made of silver, you'll find it here. This is the place embassies go to replace missing teapots and decorators go to find objets d'art for their celebrity clients. The emphasis is on household goods, but some dealers also sell jewellery.

Wer irgendetwas aus Silber sucht, wird hier fündig. Mehr als 30 Händler bieten zwischen Fingerhüten und elaborierten Kandelabern die ganze Palette an. In den Silver Vaults machen sich Botschaftsangestellte auf die Suche nach einem Ersatz für die verloren gegangene Teekanne, und Innendekorateure finden Objets d'Art für ihre prominenten Kunden. Die meisten Händler haben sich auf Haushaltswaren spezialisiert, ein paar führen aber auch Schmuck.

Avec plus de 30 marchands vendant tout, de la timbale au candélabre ouvragé, c'est le paradis de l'argenterie. C'est ici que les ambassades viennent remplacer les théières disparues et que les décorateurs dénichent des pièces rares pour leurs clients célèbres. L'accent est sur les arts ménagers, mais certains vendent également des bijoux.

**Interior:** Around 1876 the vaults of Chancery House were rented out to wealthy Londoners as strongrooms. Gradually they became the Silver Vaults, which have existed in their current form since 1953.
**Open:** Mon–Fri 9am–5.30pm, Sat till 1pm.
**X-Factor:** English silver is said to be the finest in the world – items from all epochs are available here in more than 30 shops.

**Interieur:** Die Gewölbe des Chancery House wurden 1876 als Tresorräume an wohlhabende Londoner vermietet und wandelten sich allmählich in die Silver Vaults, die in ihrer heutigen Form seit 1953 bestehen.
**Öffnungszeiten:** Mo–Fr 9–17.30, Sa bis 13 Uhr.
**X-Faktor:** Englisches Silber gilt als das feinste der Welt – in mehr als 30 Shops wird mit Stücken aller Epochen gehandelt.

**Intérieur :** Les salles voûtées de la Chancery House ont été louées, en 1876, comme salle de coffres-forts aux riches Londoniens, puis se sont peu à peu modifiées pour devenir les Silver Vaults, inchangés depuis 1953.
**Horaires d'ouverture :** Lun–Ven 9h–17h30, Sam jusqu'à 13h
**Le « petit plus » :** L'argenterie anglaise est réputée comme étant la plus fine au monde. Plus de 30 boutiques vendent des pièces datant de toutes les époques.

# Marylebone Farmers' Market

Cramer Street Car Park (off Marylebone High Street)
London W1U 4EA
☎ +44 20 7833 0338
www.lfm.org.uk
Tube: Baker Street/Bond Street

Thanks to Marylebone Farmers' Market, the area has become foodie central. At this rain-or-shine Sunday market, fresh produce, English cheeses and free-range meat and eggs come from 100 miles around and are sold by the producers directly. Artisanal breads and delicious cakes are sold here, too. Get there early: the farmers pack up around 2pm. Shop for a picnic at St James's Park for a perfect afternoon.

Dank dem Marylebone Farmers' Market ist dieses Viertel zu einem Food-Mekka geworden. Sonntags wird bei jedem Wetter frische Ware, wie Käse aus England, Freiland-Fleisch und -Eier, feilgeboten. Alle Lieferanten kommen aus einem Umkreis von 160 Kilometern, die Waren werden direkt von den Produzenten verkauft. So finden sich hier auch selbst gebackenes Brot und leckere Kuchen. Zeitig vorbeikommen: Die Bauern packen um zwei Uhr nachmittags zusammen. Ideal, um sich für ein Picknick im St James's Park einzudecken.

Ce marché dominical est devenu le repaire des amateurs de bonne chère. Le dimanche, par tous les temps, des producteurs habitant à 160 km à la ronde viennent ici vendre leurs produits frais, des fromages anglais, des œufs et de la viande d'animaux élevés en plein air. On y trouve aussi du pain et des gâteaux artisanaux. Allez-y tôt, ils replient leurs étals dès 14h. Idéal pour s'approvisionner avant un pique-nique à St James's Park.

**Interior:** The city's largest and best-stocked farmers market.
**Open:** Sun 10am–2pm.
**X-Factor:** There are numerous cafés and restaurants in the neighbourhood, where you can end your stroll around the market with a cup of coffee.

**Interieur:** Der größte und am besten sortierte Bauernmarkt der Stadt.
**Öffnungszeiten:** So 10–14 Uhr.
**X-Faktor:** Ringsum liegen zahlreiche Cafés und Restaurants, in denen man den Marktbummel bei einem Kaffee ausklingen lassen kann.

**Intérieur :** Le plus grand marché fermier de la ville et le mieux pourvu en marchandises.
**Horaires d'ouverture :** Dim 10h–14h.
**Le « petit plus » :** On pourra terminer la visite du marché dans l'un des nombreux cafés et restaurants qui l'entourent.

# Daunt Books

83–84 Marylebone High Street, London W1U 4QW
☎ +44 20 7224 2295
www.dauntbooks.co.uk
Tube: Baker Street/Bond Street

This is easily one of the most beautiful bookshops in London, housed in an original Edwardian building with oak galleries and skylights that fill the store with natural light. It has a fabulous selection of children's books, fiction, non-fiction as well as an extensive travel section that is second to none. Staff are friendly, knowledgeable and helpful. Get a novel by Jane Austen and read it in the beautiful garden on Manchester Square in front of the Wallace Collection.

Ein Gebäude aus der Zeit Eduards VII., Eichengalerien, Oberlichter, die den Raum mit Licht durchfluten: Dies ist die schönste Buchhandlung ganz Londons. Kinderbücher, Romane, Sachbücher, die Auswahl ist fantastisch; das Angebot an Reisebüchern so groß wie nirgends. Das Personal steht mit großem Wissen hilfreich zur Seite. Tipp: Einen Roman von Jane Austen erstehen und ihn im lauschigen Manchester Square, gleich vor der Wallace Collection, lesen.

Située dans un bâtiment édouardien, avec des galeries en chêne et une verrière qui l'inonde de lumière naturelle, c'est de loin la plus belle librairie de Londres. On y trouve un merveilleux choix de livres d'enfants, de romans, d'essais ainsi qu'un large rayon de livres de voyage comme on en trouve peu en ville. Le personnel est charmant, érudit et serviable. Achetez-y un roman de Jane Austen à lire dans le beau square Manchester devant la Wallace Collection.

**Interior:** London's most beautiful bookshop is housed in a building dating from the time of Edward VII.
**Open:** Mon–Sat 9am–7.30pm, Sun 11am–6pm.
**X-Factor:** Among the travel books you can also find select second-hand titles.

**Interieur:** Die schönste Buchhandlung Londons ist in einem Gebäude aus der Zeit Eduards VII. untergebracht.
**Öffnungszeiten:** Mo–Sa 9–19.30, So 11–18 Uhr.
**X-Faktor:** Unter den Reisebüchern findet man auch Secondhand-Titel, die mit viel Fachwissen zusammengestellt sind.

**Intérieur :** La plus belle librairie de Londres se trouve dans un bâtiment datant de l'époque d'Édouard VII.
**Horaires d'ouverture :** Lun–Sam 9h–19h30, Dim 11h–18h.
**Le « petit plus » :** Parmi les livres de voyages on trouve aussi des exemplaires d'occasion choisis avec beaucoup d'intelligence.

# The Button Queue

76 Marylebone Lane, London W1U 2NF
☎ +44 20 7935 1505
www.thebuttonqueen.co.uk
Tube: Bond Street

Rows and rows of browning cardboard boxes hold thousands and thousands of buttons (new and antique) at The Button Queen. It started as a market stall in South London by Mrs. Frith, who was nicknamed The Button Queen. Her son, Martyn, now runs the shop and counts American button collectors, fashion designers and costume designers amongst his loyal clientele.

In diesem Geschäft reihen sich zahlreiche braune, mit Tausenden historischen und neuen Knöpfen gefüllte Pappschachteln. The Button Queen war ursprünglich ein Marktstand in Südlondon und gehörte einer Mrs. Frith, die als „Button Queen" (Knopfkönigin) bekannt war. Heute führt ihr Sohn Martyn das Geschäft. Zur treuen Kundschaft zählen amerikanische Knopfsammler genauso wie Mode- und Kostümdesigner.

Après avoir commencé avec un étal sur un marché du sud de Londres, Mme Frith, « la reine du bouton », a ouvert sa boutique, tenue aujourd'hui par son fils Martyn. Collectionneurs américains, créateurs de mode et costumiers hantent régulièrement ses rayons croulant sous les boîtes en papier jauni, qui renferment des milliers et des milliers de boutons, nouveaux et anciens.

**Interior:** Not one square inch is left unused; the countless button boxes and holders take up all the available space.
**Open:** Mon–Fri 10am–5.30pm, Sat 10am–3pm.
**X-Factor:** A 1960s legend. You can find wonderful historical buttons here, for example, from the Art Nouveau or Victorian eras.

**Interieur:** Hier bleibt kein Quadratzentimeter ungenutzt, die ungezählten Knopfschachteln und -schalen belegen jede verfügbare Fläche.
**Öffnungszeiten:** Mo–Fr 10–17.30 Sa 10–15 Uhr.
**X-Faktor:** Eine Legende seit den 1960ern. Hier findet man wunderschöne historische Knöpfe – zum Beispiel aus der Zeit des Jugendstils oder der viktorianischen Ära.

**Intérieur :** Il n'y a plus un centimètre carré de libre. Les innombrables boîtes à boutons occupent tout l'espace disponible.
**Horaires d'ouverture :** Lun–Ven 10h–17h30, Sam 10h–15h.
**Le « petit plus » :** Légendaire depuis les années 1960. On y trouve de magnifiques boutons historiques, datant par exemple de l'époque victorienne ou de celle de l'Art nouveau.

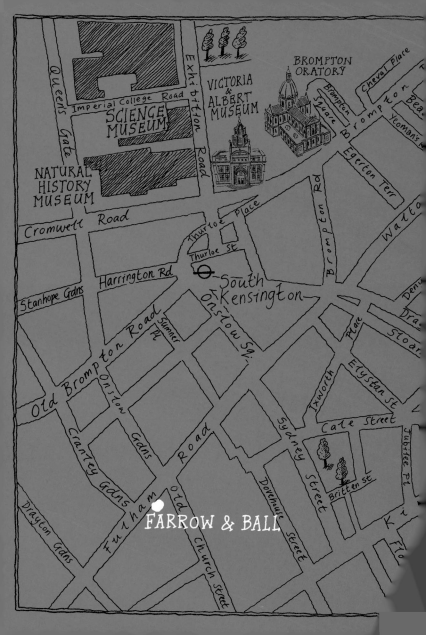

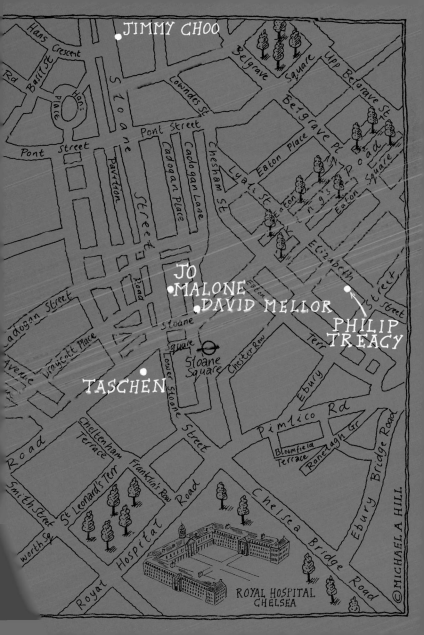

# Farrow & Ball

249 Fulham Road, London SW3 6HY
☎ +44 20 7351 0273
www.farrow-ball.com
Tube: South Kensington

Farrow & Ball is a testimony to the British talent for creating exquisite products for the home. The paint company was founded in the 1930s by chemists John Farrow and Richard Ball and all products are still made in Dorset. Farrow & Ball still provide paints for National Trust properties, but new, contemporary colours have been added to suit modern tastes. Here you can find the most subtle shades to paint your home – colours that you will not encounter elsewhere.

Die Briten sind bekannt für die Herstellung bester Haushaltsprodukte. Dazu gehören auch die Farbwaren von Farrow & Ball. Das Unternehmen wurde in den 1930ern von den Chemikern John Farrow und Richard Ball in Dorset gegründet, wo bis heute alle Produkte hergestellt werden. Es liefert die Farben für die Gebäude des National Trust. Doch man findet auch aktuelle, zeitgemäße Farben: Subtilere Farbtöne bekommt man sonst nirgends, da macht es Spaß, einen neuen Farbanstrich für das eigene Heim zu planen.

Les Britanniques n'ont pas leur pareil pour créer des produits exquis pour la maison. Cette entreprise fondée dans les années 1930 par John Farrow et Richard Ball fabrique encore toutes ses peintures dans le Dorset et fournit le National Trust, la fondation qui restaure les demeures historiques. De nouvelles couleurs modernes ont été ajoutées à son nuancier. Vous y trouverez les tons les plus subtils pour redécorer votre intérieur.

**Interior:** This shop calls itself a showroom – which is what it looks like. In the rectangular interior the graphic design of the paint cans and the range of colours really come into their own.
**Open:** Mon–Fri 8.30am–5.30pm, Sat 10am–5pm.
**X-Factor:** Farrow & Ball also print wallpapers using traditional techniques.

**Interieur:** Das Geschäft bezeichnet sich nicht als Shop, sondern als Showroom – und so wirkt es auch: Das geradlinige Interieur lässt das Grafikdesign der Farbdosen und die Farbpaletten toll zur Geltung kommen.
**Öffnungszeiten:** Mo–Fr 8.30–17.30, Sa 10–17 Uhr.
**X-Faktor:** Farrow & Ball bedruckt auch Tapeten nach traditionellen Techniken.

**Intérieur :** Le magasin ne se conçoit pas comme une boutique mais comme un showroom, et c'est ainsi qu'il se présente : l'intérieur aux lignes droites fait valoir le design des pots de couleur et les nuances de tons.
**Horaires d'ouverture :** Lun–Ven 8h30– 17h30, Sam 10h–17h.
**Le « petit plus » :** Farrow & Ball imprime aussi ses papiers peints selon des technique traditionnelles.

# Jimmy Choo

32 Sloane Street, London SW1X 9NR
☏ +44 20 7823 1051
www.jimmychoo.com
Tube: Knightsbridge/Sloane Square

Jimmy Choo has come to define everything glamorous about footwear. The flagship store on Sloane Street is also the place to find a matching bag or the right sunglasses. Whether it's a strappy stiletto or a sky-high boot, Tamara Mellon, a former accessories editor, society girl and head of the company, knows what her chic clientele – which includes Kate Hudson, Jennifer Aniston and Heidi Klum – are looking for. She started the company in 1996 with East End shoemaker Jimmy Choo, and her empire just keeps growing.

Jimmy Choo ist die Verkörperung glamourösen Schuhwerks schlechthin. In dem Flagship-Store auf der Sloane Street findet man aber auch die passende Tasche und die richtige Sonnenbrille. Tamara Mellon, Society-Girl, ehemalige Modejournalistin für Accessoires und Besitzerin des Schuhimperiums, weiß mit Riemchen-Stilettos und endlos langen Stiefeln ihre todschicke Klientel, zu der u. a. Kate Hudson, Jennifer Aniston und Heidi Klum gehören, glücklich zu machen. Den Grundstein für das erfolgreiche Unternehmen setzte sie 1996 zusammen mit dem East-End-Schuhmacher Jimmy Choo.

Jimmy Choo incarne le glamour de la chaussure. La filiale principale de Sloane Street propose aussi le sac à main assorti ou les lunettes de soleil adéquates. Qu'il s'agisse de talons aiguilles à lacets ou de cuissardes, Tamara Mellon, ancienne directrice des accessoires et grande mondaine, sait ce que veut sa clientèle ultra chic dont font partie, entre autres, Kate Hudson, Jennifer Aniston et Heidi Klum. Depuis qu'elle a créé la société en 1996 avec Jimmy Choo, chausseur issu du East End, son empire ne cesse de grandir.

**Interior:** Altogether feminine – a creamy rosé and perfect lighting. The most beautiful shoes and bags are in mirrored display cases.
**Open:** Mon–Sat 10am–6pm (Wed till 7pm), Sun midday–5pm.
**X-Factor:** Ex-Vogue editor Tamara Mellon challenges the competition.

**Interieur:** Sehr feminin in cremigem Rosé und perfekt beleuchtet. Die schönsten Schuhe und Taschen stehen in verspiegelten Vitrinen.
**Öffnungszeiten:** Mo–Sa 10–18 (Mi bis 19), So 12–17 Uhr.
**X-Faktor:** Ex-Vogue-Redakteurin Tamara Mellon läuft der Konkurrenz den Rang ab.

**Intérieur :** Très féminin dans un rose crémeux et parfaitement éclairé. Les plus beaux sacs et chaussures se trouvent dans les vitrines réfléchissantes.
**Horaires d'ouverture :** Lun–Sam 10h–18h (Mer jusqu'à 19h), Dim 12h–17h.
**Le « petit plus » :** Ancienne rédactrice de Vogue, Tamara Mellon laisse la concurrence derrière elle.

# TASCHEN

12 Duke of York Square, London SW3 4LY
☎ +44 207 881 0795
www.taschen.com
Tube: Sloane Square

The first TASCHEN Store in Britain was opened in October 2008 in Chelsea. The publisher's complete programme can be found here very close to King's Road – presented in a stylish and highly sophisticated design by Philippe Starck. With the assistance of B3 Designers and 3f Architects he has given the shop a framework of tall windows, light white curtains and dark shelves with gleaming golden crowns. This creates a perfect stage set for the shop counters of cast bronze, whose abstract shapes are reminiscent of great tree trunks.

Der erste TASCHEN-Store Großbritanniens wurde im Oktober 2008 in Chelsea eröffnet. In unmittelbarer Nähe der King's Road findet man hier das komplette Verlagsprogramm – stilvoll und sehr sophisticated von Philippe Starck in Szene gesetzt. Unterstützt von B3 Designers und 3f Architects hat er den Laden mit hohen Fenstern, leichten weißen Vorhängen sowie dunklen Regalen mit goldglänzenden Kronen eingerahmt und damit eine perfekte Kulisse für die Tresen aus Bronzeguss geschaffen, deren abstrakte Formen an mächtige Baumstämme erinnern.

La première librairie TASCHEN de Grande-Bretagne a ouvert ses portes à Chelsea en octobre 2008. Ici, tout près de la King's Road, ce store présente tout l'éventail des publications de la maison – dans un intérieur raffiné et très sélect, conçu par Philippe Starck. Avec la collaboration de designers B3 et d'architectes 3f, il a doté le magasin de hautes fenêtres, de vaporeux voilages blancs et d'étagères couronnées d'or aux teintes d'acajou foncé, créant ainsi la coulisse idéale pour les comptoirs de bronze dont les formes abstraites rappellent de puissants troncs d'arbres.

**Interior:** An elegant glass balustrade leads to the shop's own gallery on the lower floor.
**Open:** Mon, Tue, Thu, Fri, 10am–6pm, Wed, Sat 10am–7pm, Sun midday–6pm.
**X-Factor:** The new Saatchi Gallery right next door provides further enjoyment of contemporary art.

**Interieur:** Eine elegante Glasbalustrade führt zur shopeigenen Galerie im Untergeschoss.
**Öffnungszeiten:** Mo, Di, Do, Fr 10–18 Uhr, Mi, Sa 10–19 Uhr, So 12–18 Uhr.
**X-Faktor:** Weiteren und zeitgenössischen Kunstgenuss bietet die neue Saatchi Gallery gleich nebenan.

**Intérieur :** Une élégante balustrade de verre mène à la galerie souterraine du magasin.
**Horaires d'ouverture :** Lun, Mar, Jeu, Ven 10h–18h, Mer, Sam 10h–19h, Dim 12h–18h.
**Le « petit plus » :** Pour les amoureux d'art contemporain, la nouvelle Saatchi Gallery est basée juste à côté.

# Jo Malone

150 Sloane Street, London SW1X 9BX
☎ +44 870 192 5121
www.jomalone.co.uk
Tube: Sloane Square

Jo Malone launched her business out of her flat in the 1980s and her facials quickly became cult treatments with models such as Yasmin Le Bon and her friends. She opened her shop in 1994 and expanded to include fragrances – the grapefruit is delicious – and wonderfully light make-up. Products come in many price ranges and it's hard to resist the cream-and-black packaging.

Jo Malone legte den Grundstein für ihr Geschäft in den 1980ern – in ihrer Wohnung. Ihre Gesichtsbehandlungen begeisterten Kundinnen wie Model Yasmin Le Bon und wurden so Kult. 1994 eröffnete Malone den ersten Laden; gleichzeitig erweiterte sie ihr Angebot mit Düften (der Grapefruit-Duft ist himmlisch) und traumhaft leichten Make-ups. Beim Anblick der cremeweiß-schwarzen Verpackungen fällt es schwer, dem Angebot zu widerstehen.

Jo Malone a commencé dans son appartement dans les années 1980 et ses masques sont vite devenus culte auprès de mannequins comme Yasmin Le Bon et ses amies. Elle a ouvert sa boutique en 1994, élargissant sa gamme aux parfums (le pamplemousse est divin) et au maquillage léger et sublime. Il y en a pour toutes les bourses. Son packaging crème et noir est irrésistible.

**Interior:** This highly elegant interior is exclusively in white and black.
**Open:** Mon, Tue, Sat 9.30am–6pm, Wed–Fri 9.30am–7pm, Sun 11.30am–5pm.
**X-Factor:** The ten-minute hand and arm massage is a hot tip among London's power-shoppers – and it works wonders.

**Interieur:** Das hoch elegante Interieur ist in Weiß und Schwarz gehalten.
**Öffnungszeiten:** Mo, Di, Sa 9.30–18, Mi–Fr 9.30–19, So 11.30–17 Uhr.
**X-Faktor:** Die zehnminütige Hand- und Armmassage ist ein Geheimtipp unter Londons Powershoppern – sie wirkt Wunder.

**Intérieur :** L'intérieur très élégant est tout en noir et blanc.
**Horaires d'ouverture :** Lun, Mar, Sam 9h30–18h, Mer–Ven 9h30–19h, Dim 11h30–17h.
**Le « petit plus » :** Les accros du shopping raffolent du massage des mains et des bras de dix minutes. Tout simplement miraculeux.

# David Mellor

4 Sloane Square, London SW1W 8EE
☎ +44 20 7730 4259
www.davidmellordesign.com
Tube: Sloane Square

This shop is pure hedonism for those obsessed with cooking and anything to do with kitchens. David Mellor's career was launched when, in 1953, his Pride cutlery (now a modern classic) went into production, which he designed while still a student at the Royal College of Art. The Sloane Square shop has been keeping Chelsea kitchens looking gorgeous since it opened in 1969.

Wer gern kocht und viel Zeit in der Küche verbringt, wird in diesem Geschäft schwelgen. David Mellor machte sich 1953 einen Namen mit der Lancierung des Pride-Bestecks, das er noch als Student am Royal College of Art entwarf. Heute ist das Besteck ein Klassiker. Und seit 1969 sorgt sein Geschäft am Sloane Square dafür, dass Küchen in Chelsea gut aussehen.

Une boutique qui fera fondre tous les mordus de cuisine. La carrière de David Mellor a démarré en flèche en 1953, quand ses couverts Pride (désormais un classique) ont été produits en série alors qu'il était encore étudiant au Royal College of Art. Depuis son ouverture en 1969, les plus belles cuisines de Chelsea s'équipent dans sa boutique de Sloane Square.

**Interior:** The large and fine selection of tableware and kitchen utensils is presented over two floors.
**Open:** Mon–Sat 9.30am–6pm, Sun 11am– 5pm.
**X-Factor:** Should you need spoons made from horn, a fruit press or earthen-ware, you are sure to find the best items here.

**Interieur:** Die große und perfekt sortierte Auswahl an Besteck und Küchenutensilien wird auf zwei Etagen präsentiert.
**Öffnungszeiten:** Mo–Sa 9.30–18, So 11–17 Uhr.
**X-Faktor:** Ob man Löffel aus Horn, eine Saftpresse oder Töpferware braucht – hier findet man garantiert die schönsten Stücke.

**Intérieur :** Le grand choix de couverts et d'ustensiles de cuisine est présenté sur deux étages.
**Horaires d'ouverture :** Lun–Sam 9h30–18h, Dim 11h–17h.
**Le « petit plus » :** Que vous ayez besoin d'une cuillère en corne, d'un presse-fruits ou de casseroles, c'est ici que vous trouverez les plus belles pièces.

DAVID MELLOR

COOKING POTS
TABLEWARE
MINCERS
SCALES MEASURES
TINS
SIEVES STRAINERS
WOODWARE
KITCHEN GLASS
SPOONS SERVERS
COFFEE MAKERS
CORKSCREWS
KITCHEN LINEN

# Philip Treacy

69 Elizabeth Street, London SW1W 9PJ
☎ +44 20 7730 3992
www.philiptreacy.co.uk
Tube: Sloane Square/Victoria

Irish-born Philip Treacy is not just a hat designer, he is an artist. This is the view taken by his many fans who rely on his creations to make them look fabulous at Ascot. He started his business in the basement of the eccentric stylist Isabella Blow and has since designed hats for Chanel, Valentino, McQueen and Ralph Lauren. This shop opened in 1994 and nobody can resist going in to admire or – if they are feeling brave – to try on one of his splendid creations.

Der Ire Philip Treacy ist nicht nur Hutmacher, sondern auch Künstler. So sehen das die Kunden, die sich für einen effektvollen Auftritt in Ascot hundertprozentig auf ihn verlassen. Er startete sein Unternehmen im Keller der exzentrischen Stylistin Isabella Blow und hat seither Hüte für Chanel, Valentino, McQueen und Ralph Lauren entworfen. Es ist unmöglich, dort vorbeizulaufen, ohne die prachtvollen Kreationen bewundert oder anprobiert zu haben.

L'Irlandais Philip Treacy n'est pas un simple modiste, c'est un artiste. Croyez-en ses nombreux clients qui comptent sur lui pour briller à Ascot. Depuis ses débuts dans le sous-sol de la styliste excentrique Isabella Blow, Philip Treacy a dessiné des chapeaux pour Chanel, Valentino, McQueen et Ralph Lauren. On ne peut s'empêcher d'entrer dans sa boutique, ouverte en 1994, pour admirer ses splendides créations et, si on s'en sent le courage, en essayer une.

**Interior:** The glamorous and elegant interior was designed by Tom Dixon.
**Open:** Mon–Fri 10am–6pm, Sat 11am–5pm.
**X-Factor:** Hat models by this award-winning designer have also been purchased by Karl Lagerfeld.

**Interieur:** Das glamouröse und elegante Interieur stammt von Tom Dixon.
**Öffnungszeiten:** Mo–Fr 10–18, Sa 11–17 Uhr.
**X-Faktor:** Die Modelle des mehrfach preisgekrönten Designers ordert auch Karl Lagerfeld.

**Intérieur :** L'aménagement glamoureux et élégant est de Tom Dixon.
**Horaires d'ouverture :** Lun–Ven 10h–18h, Sam 11h–17h.
**Le « petit plus » :** Karl Lagerfeld commande aussi des modèles au styliste plusieurs fois primé.

PHILIP TREACY

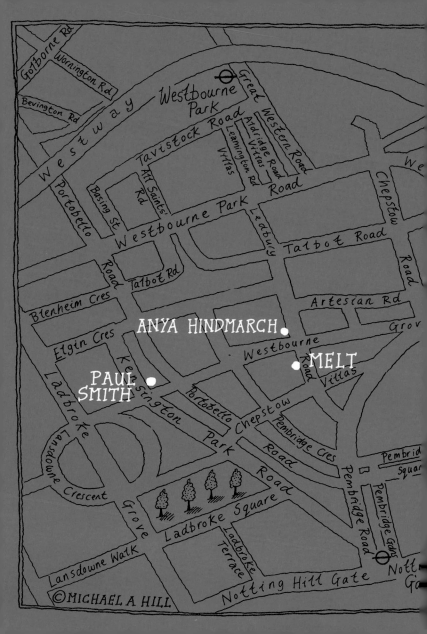

# Paul Smith

Westbourne House
122 Kensington Park Road, London W11 2EP
☎ +44 20 7727 3553
www.paulsmith.co.uk
Tube: Notting Hill Gate

This enormous villa, which was converted into a shop in the late 1990s, provides one of the most incredible retail experiences in London. In fact, it was Sir Paul Smith's shop that was instrumental in the gentrification of this area in the past decade. Over three floors, choose from Smith's finely tailored suits, feminine dresses, accessories, vintage toys and books – all quirky and very English, like Smith himself.

Aus einer riesigen Villa wird eine Boutique. In den späten 1990ern eröffnete hier Sir Paul Smith sein Geschäft und löste damit im Viertel einen Boom aus. Über drei Stockwerke verteilt, findet man seine fantastisch geschnittenen Anzüge, feminine Kleider, Accessoires, Vintage-Spielzeug und Bücher. Alles sehr eigenwillig gemischt und englisch, genau wie Smith. Eines der spannendsten Einkaufserlebnisse in London.

Cet hôtel particulier converti en boutique à la fin des années 1990 offre une expérience unique à Londres. De fait, il a sérieusement contribué à l'embourgeoisement du quartier. Sur trois étages, vous pouvez flâner entre les costumes superbement taillés, les robes féminines, les jouets anciens et les livres, tous excentriques et très british, à l'image de Sir Paul Smith lui-même.

**Interior:** The classical rooms of this town house, with stuccowork and fireplaces, have been decorated with a bit of tongue-and-cheek humour, and have become a lifestyle address. You feel as if you were in someone's home.
**Open:** Mon–Fri 10am–6pm, Sat till 6.30pm.
**X-Factor:** The accessories and the Home Collection, as well as the bespoke tailoring service on the top floor.

**Interieur:** Die klassischen Räume des Stadthauses mit Stuck und Kaminen wurden mit einem Augenzwinkern eingerichtet und zur Lifestyle-Adresse. Man fühlt sich wie in einem Privathaus.
**Öffnungszeiten:** Mo–Fr 10–18, Sa bis 18.30 Uhr.
**X-Faktor:** Die Accessoires und die Home Collection sowie der Service für maßgeschneiderte Kleidung auf der obersten Etage.

**Intérieur :** Les pièces classiques avec leurs stucs et leurs cheminées ont été aménagées avec un clin d'œil ironique et sont devenues une adresse lifestyle. On se sent ici comme dans un intérieur privé.
**Horaires d'ouverture :** Lun–Ven 10h–18h, Sam jusqu'à 18h30.
**Le « petit plus » :** Les accessoires et la home collection, ainsi que le service de la mode surmesure au dernier étage.

# Melt

59 Ledbury Road, London W11 2AA
☎ +44 20 7727 5030
www.meltchocolates.com
Tube: Notting Hill Gate

Notting Hill ladies may be famously trim but even they can't resist Melt, a shop that gives chocolate addicts no hope for reform. Started in 2006 by Louise Nason, Melt's chocolates are made on site and displayed in pristine white surroundings that only emphasise the beauty of the craft of chocolate-making by hand. The Jasmine tea truffles are particularly irresistible, but then so is everything else.

Selbst die notorisch figurbe-wussten Damen in Notting Hill können Melt nicht wider-stehen. Schokoladensüchtige kann man hier schon gar nicht mehr retten. In der mi-nimalistischen milchweißen Schokoladen-Boutique, die Louise Nason 2006 gegründet hat, kommen die haus- und handgemachten Kreationen besonders gut zur Geltung. Die Trüffeln mit Jasmintee sind ganz unwiderstehlich, alles andere jedoch auch.

Les dames de Notting Hill sont réputées pour leur minceur, mais même elles ne résistent pas à Melt, la boutique où les accros au chocolat n'ont aucun espoir de rémission. Ouvert en 2006 par Louise Nason, tous les produits sont faits sur place et présentés dans un décor à la blancheur immaculée qui met en valeur leur beauté. Les truffes au thé au jasmin sont à se damner, comme tout le reste.

**Interior:** Here the designers are not behind the minimalist interior but the new chocolate flavours: Sophie Conran, for example, invented a variation with Earl Grey tea, ginger and cranberry.
**Open:** Mon–Sat 9.30am–6.30 pm, Sun 11am–4.30pm.
**X-Factor:** Chocolate addicts can sample here to their heart's content in professional tastings.

**Interieur:** Hier stehen Designer nicht hinter dem minimalis-tischen Interieur, sondern hinter neuen Schokoladensorten: Sophie Conran zum Beispiel entwarf eine Variante mit Earl Grey, Ingwer und Cranberry.
**Öffnungszeiten:** Mo–Sa 9.30–18.30, So 11–16.30 Uhr.
**X-Faktor:** Schokoladensüchtige können dem süßen Geheimnis hier auch bei professionellen Verkostungen auf die Spur kommen.

**Intérieur :** Ici, les créateurs ne sont pas ceux qui ont fait l'intérieur minimaliste, mais les nouvelles variétés de chocolat : Sophie Conran, par exemple a imaginé un chocolat à l'earl grey, gingembre et cranberry.
**Horaires d'ouverture :** Lun–Sam 9h30–18h30, Dim 11h–16h30.
**Le « petit plus » :** Les accros au chocolat peuvent déceler les secrets qui se cachent dans les succulentes friandises au cours d'une dégustation avec un professionnel.

# Anya Hindmarch

63a Ledbury Road, London W11 2AD
☎ +44 20 7792 4427
www.anyahindmarch.com
Tube: Notting Hill Gate

You may well tell yourself you don't need any more handbags but wait until you enter Anya Hindmarch's shop and then try and resist. From washbags to tote bags, there is something luxurious in here for everyone. London society girls wouldn't be caught dead going to work without one of her leather day bags.

Mit dem Vorsatz, nicht schon wieder eine Tasche zu kaufen, kommt man bei Anya Hindmarch nicht sehr weit. Ihre luxuriöse Taschenkollektion, die vom Kulturbeutel bis zur Einkaufstasche reicht, ist einfach zu verführerisch. Das wissen bereits die Society-Töchter Londons: Ohne eine der soliden Lederhandtaschen von Hindmarch verlassen sie schon gar nicht erst das Haus.

Vous croyez ne pas avoir besoin d'un sac à main de plus ? Attendez d'être entrée dans la boutique d'Anya Hindmarch. De la trousse au fourre-tout, il y en a pour tous les goûts. Les mondaines londoniennes préféreraient mourir plutôt que d'être vues sans un de ses solides sacs du jour en cuir.

**Interior:** Small and luxurious but … almost as cosy as inside a handbag.
**Open:** Mon–Sat 10.30am–6pm, Tue till 7pm.
**X-Factor:** The handbags carried by Kate Moss, Claudia Schiffer, Reese Witherspoon and Angelina Jolie are to be found here.

**Interieur:** Klein, aber luxuriös – man fühlt sich fast wie im Bauch einer Handtasche.
**Öffnungszeiten:** Mo–Sa 10.30–18, Di bis 19 Uhr.
**X-Faktor:** Hier findet man die Handtaschen, die Kate Moss, Claudia Schiffer, Reese Witherspoon und Angelina Jolie tragen.

**Intérieur :** Petit mais luxeux, on se croirait dans un sac à main.
**Horaires d'ouverture :** Lun– Sam 10h30–18h, Mar jusqu'à 19h.
**Le « petit plus » :** On trouvera ici les sacs à main que portent Kate Moss, Claudia Schiffer, Reese Witherspoon et Angelina Jolie.

# Index

# Imprint | Impressum | Imprint

© 2011 TASCHEN GmbH
Hohenzollernring 53, D-50672 Köln
**www.taschen.com**

Compiled, Edited & Layout by Angelika Taschen, Berlin

General Project Manager: Stephanie Paas, Cologne

Photos: David Crookes, London

Illustrations: Olaf Hajek, www.olafhajek.com

Maps: Michael A Hill, www.michaelahill.com

Graphic Design: Eggers + Diaper, Berlin

Lithograph Manager: Thomas Grell, Cologne

Final Artwork: Tanja da Silva, Cologne

Text: Christine Samuelian, London

German Text Editing: Christiane Reiter, Hamburg
Nazire Ergün, Cologne

English Translation: Pauline Cumbers, Frankfurt am Main

French Translation: Thérèse Chatelain-Südkamp, Cologne
Philippe Safavi, Paris

German Translation: Simone Ott Caduff, California

Printed in China
ISBN 978-3-8365-3179-5

To stay informed about upcoming TASCHEN titles,
please request our magazine at www.taschen.com/magazine
or write to TASCHEN, Hohenzollernring 53, D-50672 Cologne,
Germany; contact@taschen.com; Fax: +49-221-254919.
We will be happy to send you a free copy of our magazine
which is filled with information about all of our books.

Photo on page 2: Frith Street, 1955 © Mirrorpix

The published information,
addresses and pictures have been
researched with the greatest of care.
However, no responsibility or liability
can be taken for the correctness
of the details. The information
may be out of date due to recent
changes, which have not yet been
incorporated. Please refer to
the relevant websites for recent
prices and details.

Die veröffentlichten Informationen,
Adressen und Bilder sind mit größter
Sorgfalt recherchiert. Dennoch kann
für die Richtigkeit keine Gewähr
oder Haftung übernommen werden.
Die Informationen können durch
aktuelle Entwicklungen überholt
sein, ohne dass die bereitgestellten
Informationen geändert wurden.
Bitte entnehmen Sie den jeweiligen
Websites die aktuellen Preise
und Angaben.

Bien que nous ayons recherché avec
soin les informations, les adresses
et les photos de cet ouvrage, nous
déclinons toute responsabilité.
Il est possible en effet que les
données mises à notre disposition
ne soient plus à jour. Veuillez vous
reporter aux différents sites web
pour obtenir les prix et les
renseignements actuels.